SOTADE OLUSEGUN
Noveldramist, Poet, Novelist, Playwright, OCP, MCTS
sotadeadeyinka@gmail.com, +2348170205448
www.amazon.com

The Anatomy of Space-time
Is cosmological space emergent or fundamental?

CONTENTS

CHAPTER ONE

The Nature of Space-time

CHAPTER TWO

The Violation of Uncertainty Principle

CHAPTER THREE

The Discrete and Discontinuous Nature of Space-time

CHAPTER FOUR

The Flipping of Time-energy Entanglement

CHAPTER FIVE

The Reality of Existence

CHAPTER SIX

Space-time as the Perpetual Motion Machine of the Universe

1.0 INTRODUCTION

Space-time is the entanglement of time-relativistic scaling to energy as an epitome of space in time intervals. By this definition, we are made to know that cosmological space is a function of time and energy. Is it right to say that cosmological space emerges as a result of entanglement of time to energy? Or is it better to say that cosmological space is the inverse interaction of time with energy? In other words, is cosmological space emergent or fundamental?

To answer the afore-stated questions, we need to fully understand the instance architecture of space-time. Space-time instance is not empty but filled with energy generated by the inverse interaction of time to energy. Therefore, cosmological space is the relativistic scaling of time to energy as space of time intervals. And as a result, cosmological space is fundamental not emergent. Even in collapsed state of zero point where energy is exhausted to collapse time-energy entanglement in such a way that time can move without being entangled to energy at a constant momentum to and from, space is still the constant momentum of time. The cosmological space can only be collapsed at central zero point of time-energy wave by energy. And since it is only collapsed to non-relativistic scaling of time to energy, then it can still be expanded by time-relativistic scaling to energy. Therefore, time, energy and space are fundamental.

If time, energy and space are fundamental, what are the things that are emergent? As time-relativistic scaling is inverse to energy by relationship, then there is possibility for energy to be narrow or low when time-scaling is wide or high. Therefore, energy must be conserved in form of mass for balanced motion. Mass formation usually causes smooth and continuous curvature or nature while particle formation implements discrete and discontinuous momentum in nature.

For mass to emerge out of space-time instance architecture, time-relativistic scaling must be wide or high while energy is narrow or low. For better understanding, we need to know how it plays out at quantum level. When time is dilated in relativistic scaling to energy, particles wavelengths are elongated and overlapped to unify as a mass of particles at low energy state (position phase of time-energy wave). But the particles' wavelengths are retracted and detached from a unified mass of particles when energy is wide or high in relativistic scaling to narrow or low time (momentum phase of time-energy wave). As a result, the smoothness and continuousness of that of the classical mass is embedded in the discreteness and discontinuousness of quantum realm and vice versa. There are classical activities in quantum realm, likewise are quantum activities in classical realm.

To prove that classical and quantum realms are interwoven or inter-related, we need to understand the direction of momentum at quantum level by applying "formula of everything" and time-energy wave pattern.

By supplying 86kg of classical mass as "m" in "formula of everything", we have:

$$\frac{dt}{dm} = Um + 4m$$

$$\frac{dt}{dm} = 2.5 \times 10^{39} (86kg) + 4 (86kg)$$

$$\frac{dt}{dm} = 2.2 \times 10^{41} + 344$$

$$\frac{dt}{dm} = 2.20 \times 10^{41}$$

With embedded suspension of "344" by "10^{38}" of zeros, we annihilate the zeros by:

$$\frac{3.4}{10^{38}}$$

$$3.4 \times \frac{1}{10^{-38}}$$

$$3.4 \times 10^{-38}$$

Since the energy worth of momentum is 2.20 x 10^{41} for classical realm, energy worth of momentum at quantum realm will be 2.20 x 10^{-41} by polarization. And since mass-worth of 344 is suspended by 10^{38} of zeros, the mass-worth of 86kg mass in classical realm is 2.20 x 10^{38} while that of the quantum is 3.4 x 10^{-38} and it is compressed by "-1.2 x 10^{-3}" as addition to have 2.20 x 10^{-41} in form of polarized signal of rectilinear momentum. To form time-energy wave pattern, time and energy evolve from the central zero point of the past by entanglement that forms mass-worth and mass of particles at both maxima and minima respectively, and then collapse into central zero point of the future.

Thus we have the generated time-energy wave pattern as:

Figure 1.1

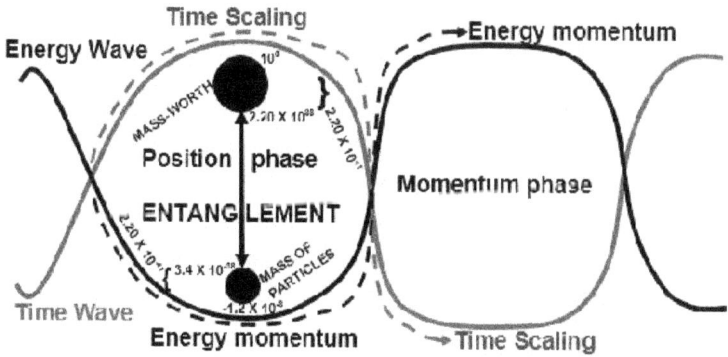

From the above illustration, energy-worth is compressed at quantum level for pressurized momentum while mass-worth remains intact at classical level. There is no external force at classical level to redirect momentum toward the central zero point (constant free fall as classical gravity). But external force is applied to redirect momentum in ascending trajectory toward the central zero point at quantum level (pressurized ascension as quantum gravity). Therefore, position phase is embedded inside momentum phase at quantum level while momentum phase is inside position phase at classical level. In other words, the direction of momentum at quantum level is outward, while direction of momentum at classical level is inward.

As a result, the mass of classical nature will be hotter and rough by boiling inside while that of the quantum nature will be hotter and rough by boiling outside. Example of such masses are Earth and Sun respectively.

Mass of particles emerges and splits from space-time like the process of multiplication of cells. However, the mass of particles is not completely detached from space-time as it is still connected by quantum entanglement and gravity.

Meanwhile, quantum mass is more solid, smooth and formed inside than the outside. The quantum mass is covered with discrete and discontinuous momentum. Example of such quantum mass is the Sun. But classical mass is more solid, smooth and formed outside than the inside. The classical mass is covered with smooth and continuous momentum, and example of such mass is the Earth. Even though quantum is characterized by discrete and discontinuous nature, it is not void of smoothness and continuousness. And even though classical is epitomized with smooth and continuous nature, it is not void of discrete and discontinuous implantation. Therefore, the curvature of space-time at quantum level may have rough edges while that of the classical level is sure to be smooth.

With afore-stated conditions and situations, we can say mass-worth and mass of particles are emergent. Even though quantum and classical realms are divergent by nature, relationship and momentum, they are compatible by mass. Therefore, spontaneous symmetry breaking point is the transiting point from classical into quantum realm.

2.0 THE NATURE OF SPACE-TIME

The question that confirms the birth of space-time as inextricable fabrics of the universe is: can space exist without the intervals of time? And if that is not so, what could have caused the intervals of time?

From the above questions, it is obvious to identify a form of energy that breeds a force which is responsible for the intervals of time. And if energy is entangled to time for relativistic scaling as hypothesized by the "formula of everything" ($dt/dm = Um + 4m$), then energy cannot be distinguished from time as non-locality is the formation of time-energy wave pattern orchestrated by quantum entanglement and gravity to form an enclosed space of the universe.

It follows that time-energy entanglement is an energy filled space of the Universe. Therefore, cosmological space is so dynamic and flexible by adjustment to cause changes that are needed for emergent development. If, as proposed by big bang theory, the universe emerged from singularity, can such minuscule point of singularity account for the vast and gigantic energy of the current size of the Universe? Or if the energy of the outburst of big bang is the total energy of this current Universe, shouldn't the Universe be retracting by now? Repulsive entanglement and gravities are the sustaining systems of this Universe.

The application of "formula of everything" reveals the flipping and intertwining of time-energy wave pattern that confirms the reason quantum and classical is incompatible. Not only that quantum and classical are incompatible by nature that spontaneous symmetry breaking violates through the "formula of everything", they are also incompatible by differences in momentum. It is also discovered that mass-worth and mass of particles are suspended at maxima (Peak Zero Point) and minima (Lowest Zero Point) of time-energy wave pattern respectively. The only point of symmetries that mass-worth and mass of particles can enter is the void (Central Zero Point).

Meanwhile, the actual state of wave particle is exposed when momentum is collapsed. The entanglement of energy to time for time-relativistic scaling from big bang singularity is the repulsion that pumps energy into the future from the past, while the quantum gravity of energy to time is the attraction of time-relativistic scaling from black hole singularity to dispense radiation into the past from the future. The action of narrow time-scaling in black hole is the inverse reaction of radiation pumped into cosmological space of the universe.

Space-time architecture is the ideal structure for cosmology and its dynamics. Energy is built by inverse interaction of energy to time in order to evolve the time-relativistic scaling through entanglements and gravities that form the cosmological space.

However, time, energy and space are fundamental but not emergent, and that is the reason the inverse relationship of energy to time must be in form of entanglement. For non-locality virtue of entanglement retains the constant momentum or motion of time in a collapsed state of time-energy independence as space, and not a state completely void of space. As a result, mass-worth and mass of particles are formed and suspended at the collapsed region of momentums as maxima point and minima point respectively. Why did mass form when momentum is collapsed? Mass-formation is feasible and stable when momentum is stable. The spinning of electrons in atoms are unified in a cold atmosphere but highly scattered in a condition where momentum is energetic. There is a convergence that occupies space even when momentum is static. Therefore, constant momentum of time in a collapsed state is a fundamental space of singularity. Time scaling will be zero at the point of singularity because energy momentum will be collapsed at that point. At singularity, there is no time-relativistic scaling to energy.

By entanglement, time is relatively scaling higher to decreasing energy as they approach their respective zero limit of maxima or minima. By gravity, the relativistic time-scaling is running lower to increasing energy as they approach the central zero point.

The afore-stated condition implies that quantum gravity increases the level of energy as time is scaling towards the central zero point (singularity of black hole). The action of quantum gravity generates a reaction of repulsion through radiation in time-relativistic scaling.

2.1 THE DERIVATION OF FORMULA OF EVERYTHING FOR TIME-ENERGY WAVE PATTERN

Formula of everything is a derived function that illustrates the entanglement of classical mass to quantum mass at maxima to minima. The interaction inside the singularity of the past emerges as time-energy entanglement through the curvy path, the fastest possible path, to maxima and minima respectively. At maxima and minima, momentums are collapsed to instantaneously form mass-worth and mass of particles respectively.

Meanwhile, the formed masses cause curvature that redirects trajectories toward the central zero point (singularity) of the future as classical gravity and quantum gravity warp the fabrics of space-time for that purpose. Therefore, the shape of spacetime is defined by entanglements and gravities.

By prior research publications of "**The Time Theory of the Universe**" (ijser.org Volume 12, Issue 10, October-2021 ISSN 2229-5518) in which the formula of everything is originally derived to satisfy the condition that fundamental energy of the Universe must evolve with time by inverse interaction to breed the gigantic energies that now form the current status of entropy of the Universe, and of "**Seeing the Anatomy of Quantum Gravity through Formula of Everything**" (ijser.org Volume 13, Issue 6, June-2022 ISSN 2229-5518)) in which time-energy wave function is derived to explore the difference in quantum momentum to classical momentum, we are thus made to know that formations of masses at low energy state are used to balance the motion of the Universe.

Similarly, Dirac (1937 – 1938) conjectured that all large numbers (Large Number Hypothesis) obtained by combining the fundamental atomic constants and cosmic parameters must be related. He thus arrived at the conclusion that the gravitational "constant" G must change with cosmic time, and he made an estimate for the change as follows:

$$\frac{F_e}{F_g} = \frac{e^2}{4\pi\varepsilon_0 G m_p m_e} \approx 2.27 \times 10^{39}$$

Meanwhile, derivation of "formula of everything" has a constant of Universe within the range of Large Number Hypothesis of Dirac. And the constant with multiplication of mass value suspends weak conveying mass by the zeros of "10^{38}" in order to entangle mass worth and mass of particles by "10^{-38}". The derivation is as follows:

Using chain-rule formula, we have;

$$\frac{dt}{dm} = \frac{dt}{de} \times \frac{de}{dm}$$

For t is a function of function of m.

Let $t = e^2$, for $t = f(e)$ where $e = m^2 + 1$.

Therefore, $e = g(m)$. Thus $t = e^2 = (m^2 + 1)^2$.

$$\frac{dt}{de} = 2 \times 1e^{2-1} = 2e$$

$$\frac{de}{dm} = 2 \times 1m^{2-1} = 2m$$

By chain rule, we have;

$$\frac{dt}{dm} = \frac{dt}{de} \times \frac{de}{dm} \quad 2e \times 2m = 4em$$

Therefore,

$$\frac{dt}{dm} = 4(m^2 + 1)m = 4m^2 + 4m$$

To induct "E = mc²" as "e" in our 4em as 4(m² + 1)m placeholder, let t = e², for t = f(e) where e = [m.c²]². Meanwhile, "4m²" and "+ 4m" are strong and weak conveying placeholders.

So, m = 274m/s² and c = 3.00 x 10⁸m/s². The speed of Sun's gravitational force and the speed of light respectively. We use the speed of Sun's gravitation as generic gravitation around with other planets orbit.

$$\frac{dt}{dm} = 4em = 4([m.c^2]^2 + 1)m$$

$$\frac{dt}{dm} = 4([274\,(3.00 \times 10^8)^2]^2 + 1)m$$

$$\frac{dt}{dm} = 4([274(9.0 \times 10^{16})]^2 + 1)m$$

$$\frac{dt}{dm} = 4([6.3 \times 10^{38}] + 1)m$$

$$\frac{dt}{dm} = (2.5 \times 10^{39} + 4)m$$

$$\frac{dt}{dm} = 2.5 \times 10^{39}m + 4m$$

The constant speed of the Universe can be denoted by capital U, and we have;

$$\frac{dt}{dm} = Um + 4m$$

Therefore, the **formula of everything** is

$$\frac{dt}{dm} = Um + 4m$$

As we can see, the constant speed of the Universe is "2.5 x 10^{39}" while that of Dirac is "2.27 x 10^{39}". However, formula of everything is a derived function of entanglement that its application and inverse counterpart is derived as follows:

$$\frac{\partial t}{\partial m} = 2.5 \times 10^{39} m/s \times 86kg + 4 \times 86kg$$

$$\frac{\partial t}{\partial m} = 2.2 \times 10^{41} + 344 = 2.20 \times 10^{41}$$

The suspended "344" by the zeros of "10^{38}" is then derived as follow to be an inverse counterpart.

$$\frac{3.4}{10^{38}}$$

$$3.4 \times \frac{1}{10^{-38}}$$

$$3.4 \times 10^{-38}$$

Both application values of "2.2 x 10^{38}" and "3.4 x 10^{-38}" are within momentums of "2.20 x 10^{41}" and "2.20 x 10^{-41}" respectively. However, "3.4 x 10^{-38}" is compressed for pressurized acceleration of quantum realm by "-1.2 x 10^{-3}".

3.0 THE VIOLATION OF UNCERTAINTY PRINCIPLE

By the nature of entanglement, time and energy exhibit non-locality as a predominant virtue. And non-locality is a pure indication of wave-pattern. Therefore, energy and time behave as wave in their entangled state before the collapsed state. They both emerge mass at their respective low energy state when collapsed near the zero point. Uncertainty principle stipulates that time spreads low when energy is spiked high, and energy spreads low when time is spiked high. The effectiveness of uncertainty principle is the justification of rough edges for mass of particles as the resolution of mass convergence is blurry or justification for non-feasibility of mass convergence for clear establishment of position. But such constraint is demolished by "formula of everything" through time-relativistic scaling that stretches energy beyond its limit threshold for spontaneous symmetry breaking.

Formula of everything ($dt/dm = Um + 4m$) violates the uncertainty principle through spontaneous symmetry breaking. By extending energy beyond its limit threshold, spontaneous symmetry breaking emerges to converge the spread particles via time-dilated scaling that is instantaneously void of entanglement. Momentum is briefly collapsed at the maxima and minima zero points of time-energy wave pattern to suspend mass-worth and mass of particles at low energy state respectively.

Meanwhile, every collapse of momentum through the zero point of maxima and that of the minima changes the course of motions toward the central zero point. Therefore, the collapsed state of momentum, or time-energy inverse interaction is a mass-converging formation for quantum gravity drive. When either time or energy collapses at maxima or minima respectively, it allows for mass formation as energy is independent of time-relativistic scaling and concentrates spread particles as a mass of particles.

Therefore, position can be obtained within a momentum at quantum level. The low energy state is embedded in quantum mass while that of the classical mass is enveloped by it. Therefore, the capturing of position and momentum is ascertained by spontaneous symmetry breaking orchestrated by "formula of everything" ($dt/dm = Um + 4m$).

To quantize by circle, p (momentum) takes the value of $h.n/R$ (where "h" is a plank scale, "n" is an integer number and "R" the radius of a circle) as a discrete value of momentum. Whereas, if R goes to infinity limit, then the separation of points on x axis goes to zero and thus change the discrete separation of points to continuous separation of points.

Therefore, a particle in infinity space can take any value for its momentum just as it could for its position. And since "formula of everything" is a derivation that extends to zero limit, then its derived momentum and position can take any value in a continuous space of infinity to form both mass of classical and that of the quantum in position phase with inverse difference of rough coverings for quantum mass and rough innards for classical mass.

It follows that 86kg mass input into dt/dm = Um + 4m (formula of everything) results to 3.4×10^{-38} as quantum position while 2.20×10^{-41} is the quantum momentum that compresses the quantum position for pressurized acceleration. Therefore, momentum covering is the outside layer of quantum mass that Scientists quantized through black body radiation.

4.0 THE DISCRETE AND DISCONTINUOUS NATURE OF QUANTIZED SPACE-TIME

Space-time by time-energy entanglement is certain to have hot and cold regions in the universe. By using time-energy wave pattern, we realize the hot regions near both singularities of central zero points of big bang and black holes.

Figure 2.1

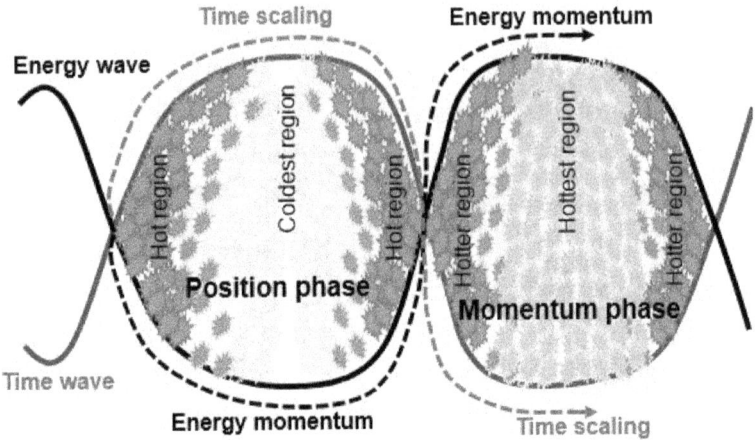

From the hot region, the temperature is running low as time is scaling higher or wider in relativistic scaling to energy that is dropping low or narrow till it gets to the maxima and minima entangled regions where high level of humidity is established to tolerate a sustainable condition for mass formations that change momentums toward the central zero point of the future. However, the temperature is starting to increase near the central zero point of the future.

Meanwhile, the temperature is hotter in momentum phase as energy is higher than the down-scaling time. At and around maxima and minima zero points, temperature is at its highest status, and so, is trajectory redirected toward the central zero point of the future.

The discrete and discontinuous nature of quantized space-time is facilitated by temperature level of time-energy entanglement. From above diagram, we can see that the core layer of momentum phase is the hottest region, while the outermost region is hotter than that of the position phase.

Meanwhile, momentum phase enshrouds position phase at quantum level as a quantum mass is generated out of time-energy entangled space-time. Therefore, curvature of space-time is tended to be rough where quantum mass emerges. As a result, the surrounding region of space-time to the quantum mass is quantized by the virtue of that roughness. For when time is dilated by scaling, wavelengths of particles are elongated to overlap each other for smooth and continuous formation of mass of particles. But when time is narrow by scaling, wavelengths of particles are shortened by retracting from each other as discrete and discontinuous particles.

Therefore, high temperature facilitates quantization of space-time through the formation of mass of particles with rough coverings and also the formation of particles of discrete and discontinuous nature.

5.0 THE FLIPPING OF TIME-ENERGY ENTANGLEMENT

The flipping of time-energy entanglement is from entanglement phase to gravity phase. This development forms a whole time-energy wave pattern that closes up two inverted cones by the open heads.

Figure 3.1

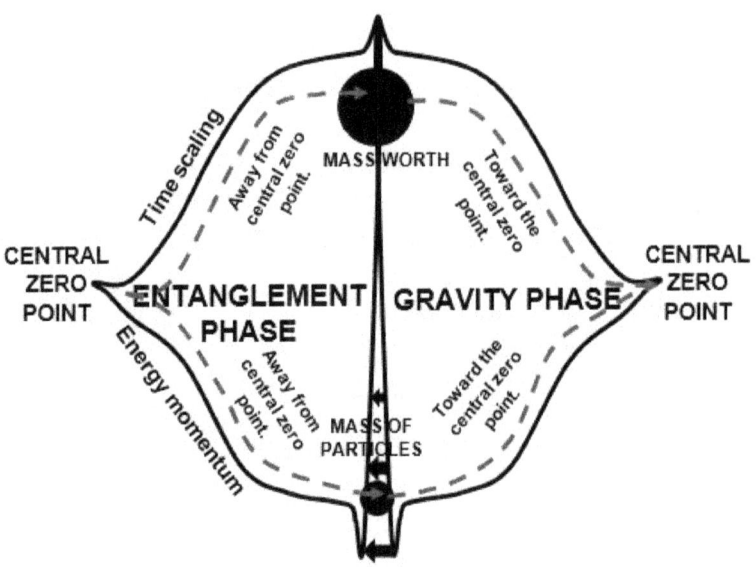

As indicated by the figure 3.1 above, the scaling of time to energy is inverse away from the central zero point, and that is the entanglement phase of time-energy wave pattern. The momentums are collapsed at maxima and minima zero points to form mass-worth and mass of particles that are entangled.

Meanwhile, the collapses of momentums now redirect trajectories toward the central zero point of the future as gravity phase. It then follows that the constant descending trajectory from maxima to the central zero point of time-energy wave pattern is the classical gravity, while the pressurized ascending trajectory from minima to the central zero point of time energy wave pattern is quantum gravity.

Quantum entanglement is an inter-sectional transition or anti de-sitter space from gravity phase. Entanglement phase is an inverse cone to gravity phase. But gravity is a de-sitter space to entanglement. Gravity is a complementary cone to entanglement phase.

It follows that quantum entanglement is the facilitator of time-travel architecture as inverse or opposed energies are essential at both classical and quantum level. At classical level, positive energy is needed towards the maxima point of time-energy wave for mass formation through energy path. Meanwhile, negative energy is needed at quantum level towards the minima point of time-energy pattern for mass of particles formation through the trajectory of energy.

5.1 THE ARCHITECTURE OF TIME TRAVEL

Since quantum gravity is fortified by positive energy of mass of particles' formation, then the whole mass is compressed by negative force for pressurized acceleration to climb toward the central zero point of time-energy wave pattern.

Quantum gravity is necessitated by a negative energy from the outside to compress the excessive mass of particles for accelerated ascension towards the central zero point of time-energy wave pattern. Therefore, the traversing energy of quantum gravity is positive while that of the classical is negative. Gravity phase is an inverted clone of entanglement phase.

Entanglement emerges away from the central zero point of the past, while gravity converges towards the central zero point of the future. Therefore, time-travel must follow the path of energy from the singularity into the future and past.

Time-travel technology should be able to foster gravity inside entanglement. For repulsive divergence of particles through entanglement must be reassembled by gravitational convergence of mass-evolving formation. Therefore, the engineering of time-travel technology requires the followings:

1. The compactness of time-relativistic scaling as a pressurized channel for 'faster than light' travel.
2. The application of 'formula of everything' as the calculation for threshold limit of entanglement and

gravity that is based on the value of classical mass.
3. The identification of energy path and transitional flipping of energy as negative in quantum realm and as positive in classical realm

However, the compactness of time-relativistic scaling is the source of the needed energy level for quantum entanglement, while formula of everything by application will specify the feasibility boundary for the operation. And energy path is the trajectory ideal for the time-travel entanglement as negative energy will sustain the collapsing particles through to the suspended point where momentum is completely collapsed for positive energy that will sustain mass formation from quantum realm through to classical level and in classical realm.

6.0 THE REALITY OF EXISTENCE

The reality of existence is established by the energy of potential value. Meanwhile, energy of a potential value can only be feasible in a vast space collapsed by the momentum of constant time-suspension.

It follows that the reality is an extremely tiny capturing of a presence made available by a vast space that smoothens out the rough edges of highly energetic momentum in a collapsed state for constantly suspended energy. Therefore, potential energy can only be established in a stable condition, a low energy state. As vast as the whole Universe is, it has a tiny presence of reality in itself.

Let say the singularity of big bang in all directions through to that of the Universe grand future is the trajectory from the past to the future (West to East), and the peak zero point (maxima) of the expanded space from North to South is the trajectory from the classical present through to quantum present. In the whole of this vastness, there is a tiny reality in the present phase of both classical and quantum when momentum collapses at maxima and minima zero points to briefly form and suspend the real mass-worth and mass of particles.

The only reality is the narrowly suspended and transiting present in vast space generated by the singularities of the past and future. Little wonder the future is a simulation of imagination while the past is a counter of expiration. Therefore, the time-relativistic scaling of speed difference is the illusive reality of the future and past. That is why speed difference of relativistic scaling could increase or decrease biological ageing.

By formula of everything ($dt/dm = Um + 4m$), it is proved that time-relativistic scaling uses energy, and space-time curvature depends on mass emergence of time-energy inverse interaction. Therefore, mass-worth and mass of particles are suspended at maxima and minima of time-energy wave pattern to implement curvature at position phase towards the central zero point of time-energy wave pattern (figure 1.1). The only area where reality is feasible in time-energy wave pattern is at the point of maxima to minima entanglement, where mass-worth and mass of particles are formed and suspended by the collapse of momentum. Other zero points in time-energy wave pattern allow particles or mass to pass through.

It follows that reality is a state of stable condition that is void of blurriness which clearly and fully displays the entirety and fundamentality of its system. And that state is the point where momentum is instantly collapsed to form and suspend mass-worth and mass of particles through entanglement. Space-time as an entanglement of time-energy wave pattern is technically lowering energy towards the maxima and minima points of time-energy wave in order to breed mass-worth and mass of particles at the point of spontaneous symmetry breaking as instantly as momentum is collapsed to establish tiniest reality of the Universe.

To prove this quick instance of reality, Let say a group of sequential pictures is quickly flipped through from the last picture to the first as the other grouped end-side is pinned down at the middle. The generated effect of this action is "motion picture" of story-telling sequence. Our perception of the flipping transitions is the motion-like simulation that transforms the reality of clear and still pictures to blurry motion pictures in extremely fast pace, and less blurry in slow pace. But the actual reality is the stable condition that warrants the still mode of pictures.

I know it might still be argued otherwise, as Earth is still in our perception, whereas it is actually moving in what may be termed reality. That brings forth the question of whether the stable state or the motion state is the actual condition for reality. But if we are to be more objective in our approach, we may settle for the "stable state" as consciousness is the concentration of separate neural circuits while scattering effect of neural circuits is termed subconscious state. I will certainly go for a state that displays an entity as a clear and stable vision any day any time.

7.0 SPACE-TIME AS THE PERPETUAL MOTION MACHINE OF THE UNIVERSE

Space-time as time-energy wave pattern indicates the possibility of negative and positive regions in the Universe. When time is high, energy is low. By the virtue of entanglement, non-locality of time and energy will make energy to be positive where time is high and negative where time is low. Therefore, entanglement is the propagation of positive energy to inner positive region of the relativistic time-scaling and propagation of negative energy to inner negative region of the relativistic time-scaling. Meanwhile, gravity is the propagation of negative energy to inner positive region of the relativistic time-scaling and propagation of positive energy to inner positive region of the relativistic time-scaling.

In that case, time-energy entanglement which results to gravity phase is the perpetual motion machine of the Universe. Inasmuch position phase of time-energy wave pattern leads to momentum phase, the combination of entanglement phase and gravity phase has the full potential to run our Universe in perpetual motion.

However, we can engineer the entanglement phase and gravity phase for perpetual motion machine that will sustain uninterruptible power supply. The system will be like that of the opening and closing valves as entanglement will open and gravity will close the system to eject highly energetic momentum. Therefore, entanglement, as a wave, propagates outwardly from the centre while gravity, as a wave, propagates inwardly to the centre. When a wave propagates outwardly, its repelling power source is from within. But when a wave propagates inwardly, its pressurizing power source is from the outside. And that explains the perpetual motion machine of the Universe as gravitational trajectories of both classical and quantum masses are combined toward the central zero point of time-energy wave pattern that serves as a singularity of compact pressure for the repulsive nature of entanglement.

To better explain the system, gravity ejects radiation as a result of the compressed nature of attraction that expands the cosmological space by entanglement which collapses repulsive momentum at the point of spontaneous symmetry breaking for recycled gravitational drive.

The question now is: what is the function of the system? The function of the system is to implement a balanced automation of sustained universe as simulated reality of life-entailed value. Space-time is the essential ground for the existence of life as interactions of entanglements and gravities are major key players to sustaining space-simulated experiences.

REFERENCES

Dirac, P.A.M.: 1937, Nature 139, 323

The Time Theory of the Universe Research Publication:
https://www.ijser.org/onlineResearchPaperViewer.aspx?The-Time-Theory-of-the-Universe.pdf

Seeing the Anatomy of Quantum Gravity through Formula of Everything Research Publication:
https://www.ijser.org/onlineResearchPaperViewer.aspx?Seeing_the_Anatomy_of_Quantum_Gravity_through_Formula_of_Everything.pdf

The Anatomy of Quantum Gravity:
https://www.amazon.com/dp/B0B49ZCYNH

The Time Theory of the Universe:
https://www.amazon.com/dp/B09K1K7Z7T

www.ingramcontent.com/pod-product-compliance
Lightning Source LLC
Chambersburg PA
CBHW071246180325
23673CB00048B/516